THE NO SCALES, JUST SONGS
VOCAL WORKOUT

A song-based method for warming up
and strengthening the voice

SUSAN ANDERS

Publisher Information:
Sweet Dreams (Are Made Of This): ©1983 BMG Songs Inc.
I'll Stand By You: ©1994 Emi April Music, Tom Kelly Songs, & Jerk Awake
Centerpiece: ©1952 Marissa Music & Andrew Scott Inc.
Unchained Melody: ©1955 Frank Music Corp.
Can't Help Falling In Love: ©1962 Gladys Music
Willow Weep For Me: ©1932 The Songwriters Guild
How Sweet It Is: ©1964 Stone Agate Music
Since I Fell For You: ©1948 Advanced Music Corp.
Dark End of the Street: ©1967 Screen Gems-Emi Music Inc.
Walk Away Renee: ©1966 Alley Music Corp & Trio Music Co Inc.
All of Me: ©1931 Marlong Music Corp.
Young At Heart: ©1954, 1984 June's Tunes & Cherio Corp.
Crazy Baby: ©1995 Songs Of Polygram International & Womanly Hips Music
Save the Best For Last: ©1989, 1992 Big Mystique Music, Emi Virgin Songs,
     Polygram International, Windswept Pacific & Moon And Stars Music

© 1999/2006 Susan Streitwieser Anders
First edition June 2000
Second edition July 2002
Third edition May 2003
Fourth edition March 2006
Published by Zanna Discs
P.O. Box 58155 Nashville, TN 37205
800-SUSAN-IS/800-787-2647
zanna@susansroom.com
www.susananders.com • www.singersworkout.com

Cover by NterDesign.com

Table Of Contents

Introduction

I've coached singers for over twenty years and have frequently seen what I call "scale phobia," when singers flat out refuse to sing scales and arpeggios to warm up before singing. I've also worked with singers who like to warm up with scales but occasionally want a break from them. Since virtually every voice I've encountered has benefitted from a good warm-up, I realized I had to come up with a viable alternative — something that could loosen up and strengthen the voice without those dreaded scales. What was needed was something I had never seen among the many vocal methods on the market: a warm-up CD of songs that gradually increased in difficulty and range. Singers that want a break from scales (or who simply refuse to sing them!) can still warm up and strengthen their voices by singing this sequence of songs. Singers who previously jumped right into singing without warming up will find singing this set of songs easier on the voice. Singers who *do* like to warm up with scales but have found it difficult to segue from exercises to songs will find that these songs make that transition much easier.

Each song works a different technical aspect of the voice, including breathing, relaxation, range expansion, resonance, placement, building volume, and diction. I picked these specific songs not only for their different technical challenges, but because I think they're great songs. They cover a range of styles, from pop to jazz to modern rock, and should suit the vocal needs of most contemporary singers. Instrument solos and long introductions have been edited out so you'll be steadily singing. I hope you like singing these songs as much as I do.

I'd like to thank the singers who tested the workout early on and gave me valuable feedback: Kristina Olsen, Penelope Todd, Chris French, J.R. Ramos, Cecily Gardner, Nina Feldman, Lisa Shapiro, Becky Sattin, Christine Kellogg, and Terence Gillespie. Ronny Schiff gave me very helpful advice as I was writing this guidebook. Thank you also to the great musicians. I'd especially like to thank my husband Tom Manche, who put in triple duty as producer, musician, and copy editor.

Foreword to the fourth edition:

This is the most recent edition of the Volume One guidebook. Since it's release in 2000 I've heard from singers all over the world who have used it with great success. In 2003 Volume Two of the vocal workout was released: it follows the same format as Volume One but uses eighteen different songs, and has been similarly received. Some singers prefer the songs from Volume One, so for those singers I've revised and updated the original Volume One guidebook to include any new vocal insights I've learned in the last few years.

How to Use the Book and CDs

You can use the CDs and book separately or together to warm up and strengthen your voice. How you use them will depend on several factors: whether you are a beginning voice student or already know some technique; if you do most of your singing in your car; if following lyrics helps or hinders your concentration; and whether you want to learn the mechanics of general voice technique or simply want to warm up and improve your voice without much instruction.

Working with the CDs

Sing along with me (or Geoffrey Tozer if you have the baritone/soprano CDs) on Disc 1 until you learn the melodies and lyrics to all of the songs. Basses will sing an octave lower than my voice, and sopranos will sing an octave higher than Geoffrey. Try the different warm-up sounds I suggest on the CD and see if they work for you—a sound that warms up one voice may do nothing for another, so you will be the ultimate judge. A warmed up voice feels flexible, resonant and strong. You should not feel much sensation in your throat at any time. If you do, you may be wearing your voice out instead of strengthening it.

Beginners especially should work with the warm-up sounds and not the song lyrics until they have built up some strength. Beginners may also need to stop after the first few songs the first day, adding songs in sequence day by day or week by week as your vocal cords get stronger.

More experienced singers can use the warm-up sounds as they learn the songs or move directly to singing the lyric. It's also fine to always use the warm-up sounds and never sing the lyric if you are solely using the workout as a vocal warm-up before singing your own songs. You may also be able to skip the first couple of songs, depending on how your voice feels. Keep in mind that most voices need more warming up in the morning than in the afternoon. If you've had some lessons and know which areas of your voice need the most attention, you can use the songs accordingly. For instance, I may skip the first song, but I might sing "Willow Weep for Me" twice to work my transition area. Until you get a feel for the songs, start from the beginning each time you use the CD, unless you use it more than once a day. In that case, you can start where you've left off. Another exception to this starting from the top rule would be those singers who warm up by singing scales and arpeggios and want to use specific songs to work specific technical areas.

Once you have the lyrics and melodies memorized you can use Disc 2 and move much faster. Unlike most karaoke CDs, I chose to have a separate CD for the music only tracks. You won't have to search the first CD to find them, nor turn down one of your speakers and lose the stereo sound to just hear the music tracks. On Disc 2 I only announce the title, the warm-up sound, and focus for each song. Disc 2 gives you more room for stylizing since it only has chords and no melody to follow. I also offer some examples of different ways to stylize at the end of Disc 2.

Singing the first nine songs of the workout should be enough to warm up your voice for the day. The second half will help you build more strength, volume and vocal dexterity. These later songs are fairly difficult and should be approached with caution. If you feel any vocal strain that isn't relieved by breathing correctly and/or singing sloppier to increase facial resonance, either take a break for half an hour or quit for the day. It's much easier on the voice to work shorter daily sessions as opposed to a long session once a week. Regular daily sessions, even short ones, are also better for building and maintaining vocal strength.

Keep in mind that while the range of these songs should fit a typical soprano/baritone or alto/bass range, every voice is different. The lowest note in the alto/bass workout is the Eb below middle C, the highest is the D almost two octaves above that. The lowest note in the baritone/soprano workout is an Ab, the highest is the G almost two octaves above that. If a note is too high or low for you to sing comfortably, try the troubleshooting suggestions in the book or find an alternate note. It's never good to force your voice where it doesn't want to go.

Working With the Book and CDs

If you would like to learn more about vocal technique in a systematic way, use the CDs in conjunction with the book. I highly recommend this approach, especially for beginning singers. I discuss a different vocal topic in each chapter, plus I troubleshoot the hard parts of each song. I've also included some expansion ideas for when you've got the songs down and want to take them further. The sequence of topics follows the same general sequence I use when I'm coaching a singer. Read the section on "Angel From Montgomery" before you listen to the CD. Try all the breathing exercises and postures, then stay aware of your breathing when you sing the first song with the music. Move through the book in this same manner, reading about each song before learning it. Move as slowly or quickly as you like. A good pace for a beginner would be to add one song and chapter a week for the first nine songs. The later songs are more advanced, so spend more time with each of them before proceeding.

Another method is to use the book only if you are having difficulty with a specific song. Read the section on that song or go straight to the troubleshooting paragraph.

Many singers find it helpful to have the lyrics in front of them while learning a song. Feel free to write in breath marks and underline problem words.

Contemporary vocal styles occasionally bend the rules of good voice technique. A singer may push his/her chest voice too high, or go for a throatier, hoarser, or overly airy tone. My feeling is that all singers should learn the rules before breaking them. So sing this warm-up with care, staying conscious of your body and never pushing or straining, even if you plan on bending the rules a bit when you sing your own songs.

Angel From Montgomery

<u>Focus:</u> Breathing
<u>Sound:</u> Mmm
<u>Alto/Bass Key:</u> B
<u>Baritone/Soprano Key:</u> Eb

     The first thing any singer must attend to is breathing, since running out of air can cause vocal strain, a weak tone, and pitch problems. The breathing we all have done since birth usually isn't sufficient for the extra demands of singing; for singing you need to take consistently full inhalations. You also need some control over the exhalation, which is when the sound is produced.

     There are a couple of schools of thought about correct breathing for singing. On the inhalation, for instance, some teachers think that you should feel some expansion in your lower belly: this happens when your diaphragm (the dome-shaped muscle that essentially bisects your midriff and works your lungs,) drops and pushes against your stomach as your lungs fill with air. This is often called diaphragmatic or stomach breathing, though no air is going into your stomach. This kind of breathing is easiest to notice when you first awaken and your body is relaxed. Another way to feel this is to slightly slouch forward in a standing position, knees bent. This relaxes the stomach, and your breathing should feel deeper. The trick is to keep your stomach relaxed and the inhalation deep when you stand up straight.

     Other teachers think instead that you should feel most of the expansion on the inhalation in your sides and lower back. Their thinking is that since your lungs wrap around to your sides, that's where you should feel the expansion as you breathe in. This is called intercostal breathing. You can usually feel this by bending over straight-backed from your hips with your head slightly raised, and with your hands on your rib cage, thumbs forward.

     A third group feels that the best inhalation is a combination of both diaphragmatic and intercostal breathing. The diaphragm drops, the lower abdomen slightly protrudes, then the rib cage expands. I usually go with what is easiest for each individual singer. I've encountered too many singers who have struggled for years to adapt to one teacher's breathing method when another method is simple to do and produces an equally deep inhalation. The critical factor is that you are not taking a shallow chest breath. Watch your chest and shoulders in the mirror as you inhale. If you see a lot of up and down movement, try both of the previously mentioned postures to get your inhalation deeper and fuller. The inhalation should feel as relaxed as possible. It's on the exhalation that the sound emerges and the singer is working the most.

     You probably felt your rib cage rise and expand on the inhalation, now keep it lifted as you exhale. This may feel like the opposite of your usual exhalation, when you let go and your rib cage falls. However, if you let go of your rib cage on the exhalation you won't have control of the air as it comes out. Try exhaling slowly through your teeth on "sss," keeping your rib cage lifted, and you'll feel your lower abdomen tighten. These are the support muscles that help you control the exhalation. Singing with them active is called supporting the sound. Some people at first also feel their lower back muscles (the latissimus dorsi) when they exhale correctly since these muscles help to hold up your rib cage. By the way, many people hyperventilate and get dizzy when they first work on their breathing. This is perfectly normal and should stop happening within a few weeks.

To re-cap, here's breathing in a nutshell:
• Relax on the inhalation, feeling expansion in your belly and/or sides and lower back.
• Keep your rib cage lifted during the exhalation, forcing your lower abdomen and diaphragm to release the air slowly.

Here are two other tricks I've found helpful: Silently mouth "uhh" as you inhale to relax the throat muscles. Your diaphragm will also relax, allowing you to inhale more deeply. Also, as you work on your breathing by itself or during a song, try swaying or walking around. This keeps the rest of your body relaxed as you develop your breathing muscles.

"Angel From Montgomery" is a fairly easy song. It's comprised of short phrases so you probably won't run out of air. The pauses in-between the phrases should give you time to pay attention to your breathing. Start by humming it until you feel some resonance (vibration) in your head, then switch to singing the words in a relaxed manner as you focus on your breathing. Pay extra attention if you're sitting and/or driving while you sing, since most singers find it a bit harder to take a deep breath when sitting.

Check out their versions of "Angel From Montgomery": John Prine • Bonnie Raitt

Angel from Montgomery

John Prine

I am an old woman
Named after my mother
My old man is another child that's grown old
If dreams were thunder
And lightning was desire
This old house would have burnt down
A long time ago

Make me an angel
That flies from Montgomery
Make me a poster
Of an old rodeo
Just give me the one thing that I can hold on to
To believe in this living is just a hard way to go

When I was a young girl
I had me a cowboy
He weren't much to look at
Just a free ramblin' man
But that was a long time
And no matter how hard I try
Those years just flow by
Like a broken down van

Make me an angel
That flies from Montgomery
Make me a poster
Of an old rodeo
Just give me the one thing that I can hold on to
To believe in this living is just a hard way to go
To believe in this living is just a hard way to go

Centerpiece

Focus: Placement, Loosening Face and Throat
Sound: Da
Alto/Bass Key: D
Baritone/Soprano Key: F

Just as a dancer stretches out her legs before working on a routine, so a singer should loosen up the different parts of the vocal apparatus as part of a warm-up. A loose jaw and mouth will make it easier to attain open vowels and to enunciate well. A relaxed face is less apt to contort on difficult notes which can cause throat tension. Throat tension can give you a constricted voice that feels and sounds tight, while a relaxed throat will allow the sound to resonate more in the face. This produces better tone and more volume. Try rolling your neck, shrugging your shoulders, and making faces prior to singing to relax all these areas.

Sloppy or mock-drunk sounds are great for initial vocalizing. Your tongue relaxes to make these sounds which then causes your throat to relax as well. This in turn allows the sound to resonate (or vibrate) more in your head and not your throat. When singers talk about "placement," they are talking about where they feel their voices resonating. As a general rule, if you feel the sound lodged in your throat when singing or speaking you may eventually experience voice problems. Too much feeling in the throat is a sign of muscle tension. You want to feel resonance around the nose, mouth, and eyes. Placement, along with correct breathing and relaxation, are key elements when you are warming up your voice. They remain important throughout any singing session.

"Da" is a good warm-up sound; the "D" keeps your tongue moving and the open "ah" stretches out your jaw. If the "da" is enunciated in a fairly loose or sloppy way most people feel some resonance in their heads. If not, try "myah" or "wa" instead. If your throat is feeling tense, try slowly shaking your head "no" as you sing, but don't do this if you're warming up while you drive!

Warming Up

• Sing "da" or "myah" in a sloppy way until your throat, face and mouth feel relaxed and loose.
• Switch to singing the lyric.

When you sing the lyric of "Centerpiece," continue the relaxed enunciation for a time, then move towards more normal singing by making the consonants crisper. Let your lips and tongue do all the work to articulate the words while your face and throat stay relaxed. Notice how the tone of your voice changes as you articulate more; it may lose a bit of richness. Alternating sloppy and normal singing can help sneak some richness back into your tone.

Since a mock-drunk sound helps to loosen the voice, singers have asked me if drinking alcohol would also work. Sorry — alcohol is terrible for your voice; not only does it dry out the vocal cords, it impairs your judgment. You may think that you are singing wonderfully when in reality you sound awful!

Potential Trouble Spots and Hints

This should be a pretty easy song to sing, as the bulk of it falls in a small range and there are no held notes requiring extra control. If you feel any throat strain spend more time singing it on "da" or "myah", or hum it.

Expansion Ideas

Since this is early on in your warm-up, hold off on stylistic ideas like runs. Runs are the extended riffs or ornamentations you often hear singers add to existing notes. Keep it simple for now.

Check out their versions of "Centerpiece": Lambert, Hendricks & Ross • Joni Mitchell

Centerpiece

Jon Hendricks & Harry Edison

The more I'm with you pretty baby
The more I feel my love increase
I'm building all my dreams around you
Our happiness will never cease
'Cause nothing's any good without you
Baby you're my centerpiece

We'll buy a house and garden somewhere
Along a country road apiece
A little cottage on the outskirts
Where we can really find release
'Cause nothing's any good without you
Baby you're my centerpiece

Sweet Dreams (Are Made Of This)

Focus: Initial Higher Notes
Sound: Blah
Alto/Bass Key: Bm—Dm
Baritone/Soprano Key: Em—Gm

When you are breathing correctly, your throat and face feel relaxed, and the sound is resonating in your face, you can start to cover a larger range of notes. At this point you may still want to keep a relaxed attitude about precise pitch, which for many singers is easier said than done. Of course we all want to sing in tune, but it's too easy when you are first warming up to go for precision and subsequently tighten your throat. Wait until later to focus on pitch; for now you can still slide around the notes a bit. The exception to this would be any singers with severe pitch problems, those that are wildly out of tune. If you don't know, a musical friend or teacher could tell you. If that's the case, you'll want to spend more time learning the right notes before progressing to other technical issues.

For many singers, high notes are harder to sing than low notes. Most of us don't speak high in our vocal range so these notes are used less. This means that warming up high notes is important. Un-warmed up singers sometimes grab at or yell high notes, constricting the throat. It's true that the vocal cords are shortening to vibrate faster and achieve the higher notes, but that doesn't mean that the muscles around the vocal cords need to get involved. When initially moving to higher notes, try to stay out of the way of your voice. If you let them, your vocal cords can comfortably create sounds in a much wider range than where you speak. That means keeping your throat and face relaxed as you did with "Centerpiece" while you gradually ascend to higher notes.

Warming Up

• Sing on "blah-blah" in a sloppy way, similar to your approach for "Centerpiece." Your throat should feel relaxed throughout the song.
• Sing the lyric.

By the way, if you ever find out why Annie Lennox didn't call the song "Sweet Dreams Are Made Of These," which is how she pronounces it, please let me know.

Potential Trouble Spots and Hints

The song modulates a key higher with every verse. If the higher keys are uncomfortable, either skip them or revert to singing them on "blah." You could also try occasional tongue rolls, a rapid dddd sound. Not everyone can do these, but if you can they are good tongue and throat loosening sounds to make. Do them over the melody or in-between phrases if your throat feels tight.

Check out the version of "Sweet Dreams" by the Eurythmics

Sweet Dreams (Are Made Of This)

Annie Lennox & Dave Stewart

Sweet dreams are made of this
Who am I to disagree?
I travel the world and the seven seas
Everybody's looking for something

Some of them want to use you
Some of them want to be used by you
Some of them want to abuse you
Some of them want to be abused

Sweet dreams are made of this
Who am I to disagree?
I travel the world and the seven seas
Everybody's looking for something

Some of them want to use you
Some of them want to be used by you
Some of them want to abuse you
Some of them want to be abused

Wade in the Water

Focus: Low End Placement
Sound: Le or Me (Ma or La on highs)
Alto/Bass Key: Bm—Abm
Baritone/Soprano Key: Em—Dbm

For some singers, getting control of their low notes is harder than opening up their high notes. The vocal cords vibrate more slowly the lower you sing, and as they relax it's easy to lose control of the note. The note can wobble, dip in pitch or become overly breathy. Low notes can also feel like they're seated in your throat. The key to controlling low notes is placing the resonance into your face and out of your throat. The various resonance spots of your head include the hard palate (the roof of your mouth), soft palate, sinus cavity, and mask area (around your eyes and nose).

It bears repeating that singing in your throat will tire your voice and cause pitch and control problems. You may find that different vowels resonate in different areas of your head. As long you feel the note somewhere in your hard palate, mouth or mask area, and not in your throat, you will build and retain control of your lower register.

Warming Up

Certain sounds tend to vibrate more in your face, making facial placement easier. Humming is the buzziest of the sounds, so if you can't get the lower notes of "Wade in the Water" out of your throat:

• Hum them for a week.

• Next, sing all except the second half of the second line on "me" or "le."

• On the second half of the second line (where the high notes are) sing "ma" or "la." This puts open vowels on the high notes and closed vowels on the low ones.

"Ee" is a closed vowel, which means your jaw is almost shut as you sing it. Closed vowels are more facially resonant and easier to control, so they are the best sounds for warming up the low end. Conversely, open vowels like "ah" are easier to sing on high notes. This is helpful to remember if you are a songwriter. Open vowels on the high notes and closed vowels on the low notes will make your song much easier to sing.

• If singing the low notes on "me" or "le" feels out of control, try slightly smiling as you sing. This tightens your tongue, which gently tightens your vocal cords.

• Try to sing with no vibrato on the low notes; this too will help you maintain control.

When you switch to the lyric of "Wade in the Water," the facial resonance will lessen in intensity, but should still be present. If it isn't:
• Try alternating from the lyric to "me" until you feel that the lyric is also resonating in your head.
• Tilt your head down about an inch, smile, and sing the lyric.

Potential Trouble Spots and Hints

• The refrain of "Wade In The Water" is repeated several times, moving down a half-step each time to gradually work the lower notes of your range. That means the highest notes occur in the first refrain. The "wa" of water in the second line has the song's highest note. Make sure to drop your jaw on it and keep your throat relaxed. Feel free to "scoop" the high note by sliding up to it from the previous note if that feels more relaxed. Scooping can easily be overdone on songs but as a warm-up method it can promote elasticity.
• "Water" in the last line covers the lowest notes. If it feels out of control or wobbly, either close your mouth a bit, smile, or make your tone a little more nasal.
• You can also avoid the lowest note by singing only the first of the three notes on the "wa" of "water."

Expansion Ideas

Gospel songs like this are wonderful for exploring note variations and ornamentations, and there is definitely room to experiment on "Wade in the Water." Beginning stylists should start with simple one- or two-note variations on any held note in the song. For instance, sing the first note of the song, go a scale step down, then return, all on "Wade." This is called a neighboring tone. Neighboring tones can be a scale step above or below the starting note.

More advanced improvisers can explore pentatonic scales, which are the basis for many gospel, pop, and R&B runs. See the glossary for more about pentatonic scales. Also try copying individual runs from other singers and songs and see if they work on "Wade in the Water," or any other songs in the workout.

Check out their versions of "Wade in the Water": Andrae Crouch • Kathy Mattea

Wade in the Water

Traditional

Wade in the water
Wade in the water, children
Wade in the water
God's gonna trouble the water

I'll Stand By You

<u>Focus:</u> Working with Simple Vowels
<u>Sound:</u> Yeah
<u>Alto/Bass Key:</u> C
<u>Baritone/Soprano Key:</u> F

By now your voice should be fairly loose in the low and middle parts of your register. It's time to approach some higher notes. As I mentioned in the last chapter, for most singers it's easier to hit high notes on vowel sounds where the jaw is dropped. When you drop your jaw, your throat opens and your soft palate, that arch at the back of the roof of your mouth that lifts when you yawn, raises a little. This brings more sound vibration into your sinus cavity and makes it easier to sing higher notes.

The jaw and tongue work in conjunction with the vocal cords. Actually, the vocal cords are folds of muscle and tissue, not cords like a guitar string. You can't control the muscles of the vocal cords the way you can move your fingers, but you do have control over your mouth, tongue, jaw, and soft palate; these in turn affect the vocal cords. Every vowel you sing has an optimal jaw position that makes the note easier to sing. For example, sing the vowel "Ee" with your teeth and lips just parted. Now sing it again with your jaw fully dropped. You'll feel that it's much more difficult the second way.

Most vowel sounds are simple vowels: you put your jaw and lips in the right position and you get the sound. For all of these vowels your tongue should be relaxed but firm, resting behind and touching the insides of all your lower teeth. Here are the simple vowels and how best to shape them:

Vowel	Jaw Position	Lips Position
ee (see)	closed	slight smile
oo (too)	closed	forward
ih (this)	closed	relaxed
eh (bet)	halfway open	slight smile
ou (book)	halfway open	forward
uh (dud)	halfway open	relaxed
a (cat)	halfway open	smiled
ah (hot)	fully open	slight smile
aw (lawn)	fully open	forward

By "fully open" I mean dropping your jaw about two little finger widths.

Most of the singers I've coached needed to open up a bit more on the "ah" vowel. However, try not to overly drop your jaw and hyper-extend the muscle, which can overwork your jaw muscles, leave you sore, and even contribute to TMJ, a chronic jaw disorder.

By "slight smile" I mean just that, barely the hint of a smile. You should look interested, not like you just won the lottery. Spread that smile just slightly more for an a (as in cat) vowel. You might swallow the sound if you smile too broadly. Instead, use the "inner smile" I discuss in the "Since I Fell For You" section.

Warming Up

As I mentioned before, notes on closed vowels are usually easier to control, while notes on open vowels feel more open and relaxed. Singers are always searching for the balance of relaxation and control as they sing. "Yeah" (rhymes with cat) is a halfway open sound that for many singers is open enough to feel relaxed but closed enough to easily control the note.
• Sing "I'll Stand By You" on "yeah" until all the notes (especially the high ones) feel relaxed. For a small percentage of singers "yeah" is not a comfortable sound. If this is the case, use "yah" instead.
• Sing the lyric.

Potential Trouble Spots and Hints

In "I'll Stand By You," the hardest notes to hit are the highest. Happily, many of these notes are on words with open or halfway open vowels.
• Let your jaw drop and notice how it's easier to sing the words "sad" and "cry" in the first verse, and "stand" in the chorus.
• For the rest of the song, notice what your mouth is doing on all of the high notes and see if any adjustments make these notes easier to sing. Watch out for the word "stand" in each chorus which often falls on a high note. Hopefully, the singing you did on "yeah" prepared you for it.
• There are many ascending lines in the verse. Some singers find ascending melodies more difficult to sing than descending. If that's the case for you, make sure that your breath support muscles are active and keep your jaw loose.
• The word "you" that falls on a high note in the final chorus is a closed vowel and may be difficult to hit. Drop your jaw a bit more and see if it becomes easier to sing. Slightly puckering your upper lip can also help. The higher you sing in any song, the more you should drop your jaw and open the vowels, even (and especially) on the closed vowels. If "you" continues to be problematic, replace it with "yeah" or "yah" until you've built more strength in your vocal cords.
• "I'll Stand By You" has some words on higher notes that aren't so simple to sing, like "cry" and "don't." These are words that have diphthong vowels, which I discuss in the next chapter.

Expansion Ideas

An appoggiatura is like an upper neighboring tone without the first of the three notes. For example: Sing "I'll stand by you" adding an upper neighboring tone on "you." Now sing it again, but start on the neighboring tone (the second of the three notes), then sing down to the melody note. Appoggiaturas aren't the easiest ornaments to master, but they're very effective for all contemporary styles.

Check out the version of "I'll Stand By You" by the Pretenders

I'll Stand By You

Chrissie Hynde, Tom Kelly & Billy Steinberg

Oh, why you look so sad?
The tears are in your eyes
Come on and come to me, now
And don't be ashamed to cry
Let me see you through
'Cause I've seen the dark side, too
When the night falls on you
You don't know what to do
Nothing you confess
Could make me love you less

I'll stand by you, I'll stand by you
Won't let nobody hurt you
I'll stand by you

So, if you're mad, get mad
Don't hold it all inside
Come on and talk to me now
Hey, what you got to hide?
I get angry too
Well I'm a lot like you
When you're standing at the crossroads
Don't know which path to choose
Let me come along
'Cause even if you're wrong

I'll stand by you, I'll stand by you
Won't let nobody hurt you
I'll stand by you
Baby even to your darkest hour
And I'll never desert you
I'll stand by you

Unchained Melody

<u>Focus:</u> Diphthongs
<u>Sounds:</u> Way, Why, Wow, Wo, Boy
<u>Alto/Bass Key:</u> D
<u>Baritone/Soprano Key:</u> G

  Diphthongs are vowel sounds created by combining two vowels: an open vowel followed by a closed vowel. In a simple vowel you put your mouth in the correct position and there it is. In a diphthong, however, the mouth has to move to complete the vowel sound. For instance, say the long "I" vowel (as in "wise") very slowly and you'll hear "ah + ee." Diphthongs are common trouble spots because if they aren't pronounced correctly they sound twangy and there is a tendency to swallow the sound. This makes high notes particularly difficult to reach. With practice, diphthongs become automatic. Here are the diphthongs English-speaking singers use:

<u>Diphthong</u>	<u>As in</u>		<u>Open Vowel</u>		<u>Closed Vowel</u>
long I	wise	=	ah	+	ee
Ow	now	=	ah	+	oo
long A	yay	=	eh	+	ee
long O	no	=	aw	+	oo
Oy	boy	=	aw	+	ee

  The style of music you sing will determine how much emphasis is placed on the open versus the closed vowel of a diphthong. Country singers, for instance, lean on the closed vowel to get their characteristic twang. Emphasize the "ee" vowel as you sing or slowly say the words "I went away" (Ah-EE went a-weh-EE) to hear what I mean. Musical theater singers often articulate both parts of the diphthong. For example: "Ah-ee could have danced all nah-eet." In most other contemporary styles the open vowel is stressed. Some singers relax the closed vowel. In fact, it's not uncommon for rock and blues singers to drop the closed vowel altogether. Think of how the word "baby" is pronounced in the blues: beh-buh, not beh-ee-bee. If you *are* enunciatating the closed vowel of the diphthong, remember to always move smoothly from open to closed.

<u>Warming Up and Working with Diphthongs</u>
• Try singing entire sections of "Unchained Melody" using only the "why" sound from the diphthong list above.
• Then use "wow," "way," etc.

• "Wo" and "boy" are the hardest. Remember to drop your jaw and let your lips come forward for the "aw" vowel. The front and sides of your tongue should rest against your lower teeth as your lips move forward.

Potential Trouble Spots and Hints

• Some words with diphthongs to watch for in this song are: "oh" at the very beginning and "night" at the end of the first verse; "time," "goes," "by," and "mine" in verse two.
• Since this is a pop song, try to emphasize the open vowel and just hint at the closed vowel.
• Because of the many held notes in the melody, this is also a good song for working on sustenance and control. Keep the low notes placed and open up on the high notes. On the sustained notes, feel where your mouth needs to be in order to hold the vowel in place with the minimum amount of effort. Then, notice where the sound resonates in your head.
• See "Dark End of the Street" for hints on increasing sustenance, and "Wade in the Water" for information about low end placement.

Expansion Ideas

The extended notes on "Unchained Melody" make it a good song for experimenting with note variations. Try three-note passing tones: sing the first note of the song on "oh" and sing two more notes up the scale. That note will also fit the chord. On "love" try a descending passing tone. Find potential ornament spots throughout the song and see if you like them better with the addition of descending or ascending passing tones. Descending passing tones show up more often than ascending ones in most styles of music and often sound a bit less showy. A three or four-note passing tone will get you from one note in a chord to another note in the same chord, but if you listen to other singers you won't hear many four-note passing tones. Instead, one of the four notes is skipped so that it's still three notes.

Check out their versions of "Unchained Melody": Righteous Brothers • LeAnn Rimes

Unchained Melody

Hy Zaret & Alex North

Oh my love, my darling
I've hungered for your touch
A long lonely time
Time goes by so slowly
And time can do so much
Are you still mine?
I need your love
I need your love
God speed your love to me

Lonely rivers flow to the sea, to the sea
To the open arms of the sea
Lonely rivers sigh "Wait for me, wait for me"
I'll be coming home
Wait for me

Oh my love, my darling
I've hungered for your touch
A long lonely time
Time goes by so slowly
And time can do so much
Are you still mine?
I need your love
I need your love
God speed your love to me

Can't Help Falling In Love

Focus: Diphthongs, Looping, "R" & "L", Vibrato
Sound: Why, Wow, Way
Alto/Bass Key: C
Baritone/Soprano Key: F

We've spent some time looking at simple vowels and diphthongs, and not much time with consonants (all the remaining sounds). There's a reason for this: on a vowel, the sound is projecting from your mouth, while most consonants cannot be sustained. Try sustaining the consonants "D," "B," or "T" and you'll understand. Except for a few musical styles (punk rock and certain musical theater character styles, for example), the singing voice is continuous, not choppy, so the emphasis is on the vowel. The consonants aren't ignored, of course, but they shouldn't impede the flow of the sound. At this point in the warm-up, continue to focus more on vowels than consonants.

An easy way to get the maximum time on each vowel is called "looping." In looping, the last consonant in a word is carried over to the next word. Here's how the first line of "Can't Help Falling In Love" looks when it's looped:

"Wah-ee zmeh nseh-ee oh-nly foo lzruh shin"

It sounds funny to speak it, but sing it that way and you'll hear how the lyric flows.

There are four consonants that can be sustained: "R," "L," "M" and "N." ("S" and "Z" are sibilant sounds that aren't counted.) Of these, only "R" and "L" can be troublesome, and usually only when they fall at the end of a word. Most of us pronounce "R" and "L" by curling the front of our tongues when we start a word, but when "R" and "L" are at a word's end we curl up the back of our tongues. This can cause a swallowed or twangy sound that only seems to fit in traditional country styles. If you listen to a range of singers you'll hear a huge difference in how much an end-of-word "R" or "L" is enunciated. In styles where the closed vowel of the diphthong is virtually dropped, like rock, "R" and "L" are just hinted at. Listen to the style of music you sing the most and find out what's appropriate. In certain wide-open styles like alternative rock or modern jazz it's ultimately the singer's artistic choice. If you choose to clearly enunciate "R" or "L," make sure you do it without swallowing the sound.

Potential Trouble Spots and Hints

There are many sustained words with diphthong vowels in this song: the first three words ("Wise men say") have two diphthongs—can you find them? It's your artistic choice how much to emphasize the two vowels that make up each diphthong, keeping in mind that unless you're doing a country version you shouldn't overdo the closed vowel. Try smoothly gliding from the open vowel to the closed so it won't sound like "Wah-eeze mehn seh-ee."

<u>Expansion Ideas</u>

Now is a good time to experiment with your vibrato—that's the (hopefully) intentional wavering or oscillating of a note. For most contemporary singing styles the standard use of vibrato is to bring it in on the last note of each phrase. However, "Can't Help Falling In Love" contains so many sustained notes that you could gracefully add vibrato to several notes within a phrase. Try adding vibrato as you are closing your jaw to complete a sustained diphthong word such as "wise," or "say" in the first phrase.

If your vibrato sounds uneven or wobbly, warm up for a time without vibrato, particularly on low notes. This will build strength in your vocal cords which eventually will help you to sustain notes with an even, non-wobbly vibrato. Use sounds with closed vowels like "me," which will be easier to control. Shaping all vowels correctly, which was discussed in the two previous chapters, will build control and strength. This will enhance your ability to increase or decrease your vibrato.

If you have no vibrato and are a beginning singer, don't panic. It can take up to a few years for a vibrato to show up, and it usually appears when you aren't trying. If you want to build a vibrato, sing an extended note on one pitch, very gradually reducing the volume without letting your voice get airy. Try this on the vowels "ee," "oo," and "ah," and try several different notes. If nothing happens, try the exercise again every month or so and don't worry about it. Lots of famous singers are doing fine without any vibrato.

Check out their versions of "Can't Help Falling In Love": Elvis Presley • UB40

Can't Help Falling In Love

George Weiss, Hugo Paretti & Luigi Creatore

Wise men say only fools rush in
But I can't help falling in love with you

Shall I stay — would it be a sin?
If I can't help falling in love with you

Like a river flows surely to the sea
Darling, so it goes
Some things are meant to be

Take my hand, take my whole life too
For I can't help falling in love with you
I can't help falling in love with you

Willow Weep For Me

Focus: Register Navigation
Sound: Yah
Alto/Bass Key: E
Baritone/Soprano Key: Ab

As you sing higher and lower in your range you may feel or hear your voice go through different areas or "registers" as the muscles in the larynx make adjustments to attain the notes. A yodel is an obvious example of a voice moving from one register to another with a marked difference in sound. Classical singers know it as the "passagio." Some lucky singers move smoothly from low to high and back, while many of us notice bumps, breaks, or sudden changes in sound quality. For most contemporary styles the singer wants a smooth transition between the registers, and an open, consistent tone throughout the range. Some teachers avoid the naming of registers in the interest of promoting the concept that "it's all one voice." While that certainly is the ultimate goal, I think it's helpful to know about the different registers.

Many contemporary singers, both male and female, sing mostly in their chest voices. These are the lower notes in your range, the register most of us use when we speak. With a few higher note exceptions, the bulk of the workout songs up until this point should be sung in chest voice. If not, they may sound very light and airy. As you sing higher, you reach a point which is too high for the chest voice to go and your vocal cords either smoothly or clumsily shift to an upper register. This register is usually called the head voice since it resonates higher in the head than the chest voice. Just to confuse matters, men usually know it as the "falsetto". Some sopranos vocalize only in head voice, some sing in both chest and head voice, and some also use their "mix" register, which I'll explain in the next chapter. Some female beginning singers and singers of both genders who haven't reached puberty may sing mostly in head voice in a lower part of the range where chest voice might ultimately be stronger. If this is the case for you, don't try to force more of a chest voice to emerge, let it come naturally over time as your voice develops.

Most adult male singers will sing all the workout songs up to this point in chest voice. The remaining workout songs should fall in a chest or mix register for the men. As the songs in the workout move to higher keys, female singers will use more and more mix *or* head voice. On "Willow Weep For Me," male singers will strive for relaxed high chest tones, while women will work on smoothing any register bumps. High tenors using the alto version who want to develop a falsetto can use the following approach.

"Yah" is a good sound for initially approaching high notes and for helping the voice move from high to low and back again without a break. The "ah" vowel causes the soft palate to lift and open the throat, while the "Y" adds a bit of helpful nasality, adding resonance and keeping the tone from being too breathy. Try sighing a long "yah" (I call this a "yawn-sigh") that goes from comfortably high to comfortably low in your range. Notice the lifting of your soft palate. It doesn't take long to develop a smooth yawn-sigh, but when you add in specific notes the voice can tense up, causing bumps or breaks. These bumps can be smoothed out with practice. Whether singing a loose "yah" or sighing it over the melody of "Willow Weep For Me," make sure that your jaw stays dropped and your tongue rests against your lower teeth. Your jaw can close up a little for the low notes but not so much that "ah" becomes "uh."

Working Out Bumps In "Willow Weep For Me"

• Maintain the feeling of sighing or sliding as you sing "yah" through the song.
• Sing each phrase with one extended "ya-ah," then try one "yah" per syllable.
• When the song feels fairly smooth, switch to the lyric, continuing to slide between the notes.
• On "Willow," "Willow," and "Bend your," the beginnings of the first three lines, you can really go for the yawn-sigh feeling you got earlier. "Listen to my plea" is another good phrase to go for that sighing feeling.
• Finally, find the balance between sliding and precise pitch that seems right for the song. If you notice any new bumps, go back to sliding and gradually add in more pitch accuracy. This can take a while; be patient with your voice.

Another way you can help your voice through transition areas is to relax and exaggerate your enunciation at the same time. It's almost like you are chewing as you sing. This relaxes your tongue which in turn relaxes your throat, making it easier for your vocal cords to make adjustments. Just as above, if this works for you you'll then need to gradually work back to a less sloppy sounding version.

Potential Trouble Spots and Hints

Two rising melodies in the bridge, "Whisper to the wind" and "Murmur to the night," may be difficult since ascending melodies require a bit more strength and support. Stay aware of them and drop your jaw on the last note of each phrase, even the closed vowel of "wind."

On the last phrase of the bridge ending with "all alone," it's easy to forget to breathe, zip right into the next phrase, then run out of breath mid-phrase or even mid-word. Either catch a breath between "all alone" and "oh," or take a deep breath after "leave my heart a-sighing" and make it last through "Oh, weeping willow tree."

Expansion Ideas

Some of the expansion ideas from previous songs will work here. You could try neighboring or passing tones on the many sustained notes. Another variation is a "throb," or double attack on the same note. Hit one of the sustained notes in the song, quickly let up on the air pressure, then reapply the pressure for a throbbing sound. Use your abdominal muscles, not your throat, to control the throb. It's easy to overdo throbs, so use them sparingly.

Check out their versions of "Willow Weep For Me": Ella Fitzgerald • Dinah Washington

Willow Weep For Me

Ann Ronell

Willow weep for me
Willow weep for me
Bend your branches green along the stream that runs to sea
Listen to my plea
Listen willow and weep for me

Gone my lover's dream
Lovely summer dream
Gone and left me here
To weep my tears into the stream
Sad as I can be
Hear me willow and weep for me

Whisper to the wind and say that love has sinned
To leave my heart a- breaking
And making a moan
Murmur to the night to hide her starry light
So none will find me sighing
And crying all alone, oh—

Weeping willow tree
Weep in sympathy
Bend your branches down along the ground and cover me
When the shadows fall
Bend oh willow and weep for me

How Sweet It Is (To Be Loved By You)

<u>Focus:</u> The "Mix" Register
<u>Sound:</u> Nyeah, Yeah
<u>Alto/Bass Key:</u> Eb
<u>Baritone/Soprano Key:</u> *G*

In the last chapter I talked about the chest and head registers. There is also an area where the chest and head registers overlap that is variously called: the cover tone, the blend, the mix, the middle register and most confusingly, the head voice. Whatever you call it (I'll call it the mix), bringing this register out in your voice is very helpful. When done right it feels and sounds like a slightly thinner version of your chest voice. Male singers can move into a mix to extend their range without cracking. Female singers can either use the mix to bring more of a "chesty" sound to their high end, or as a bridge between their chest and head registers. Developing a mix can add strength, depth, and elasticity to your high notes. Check out Marvin Gaye's version of "How Sweet It Is" and you'll hear him moving effortlessly between his chest and mix registers. Other singers with great mix registers include Natalie Cole, Rod Stewart, Ella Fitzgerald, and Steve Perry.

"Nyeah" is a whiny nasal sound that brings out the mix register and helps the vocal cords move through the full vocal range without bumps. Try saying it on some random notes, both low and high. You should sound like a bratty little kid, and you should feel it resonate behind your nose and in your soft palate. If you feel throat tension, try using the sound "nay" instead, or nod your head no as you sing to release your throat. As you sing higher notes the resonance should move straight up your head, not forward. It's not a pretty sound, but it works well in developing stronger high notes. Once established, you can work towards a more open, less nasal sound.

The mix register comes easily for some singers and can take years to develop in others. While the chest and head registers are usually easy to feel and identify, the mix can be more nebulous. It will feel easier to sing on high notes than the chest voice, and have more depth than your head tones.

The point where the voice moves into a mix can vary from singer to singer. Tenors and baritones usually shift at about F or F# above middle C, though sometimes as low as Db. Basses usually shift around Db to Eb. Altos and Sopranos can shift into a mix anywhere from A above middle C to C#, then into a head voice at F or F# above that. However, some singers of both genders feel that their mix extends to the highest note in their range. Because a chest or a mix vocal sound is what we hear in most other contemporary styles these days, songs for female singers rarely go above that F/F# switch-to-head voice point. You will still hear some nice high notes in all contemporary styles, so it pays to work those highs. Stay aware of the high chest notes just before your mix point: those are the easiest ones to yell or push.

Smoothing Register Bumps on "How Sweet It Is"

• Sing the song on "nyeah." If you want, you can stretch one "nyeah" over two or three notes.
• When you can sing the whole song on "nyeah" with no significant bumps, switch to the more open (but still slightly nasal) sound "yeah."
• If everything feels smooth, try singing the lyric.
• Do all three versions at a medium volume. Singing too loud can push your chest voice too high, causing strain. Singing too softly will bring out your head register instead of the mix. What we're after here is the mix.

Potential Trouble Spots and Hints

The first notes of each verse are the highest in the song. Stay aware of them, stay relaxed, and make sure you have enough breath support. The high notes in the first verse may be more difficult than the second because many of them fall on closed vowel words like "needed " and "you." Drop your jaw a bit on these and imagine the sound arcing up through your soft palate and out through your eyes.

The rhythm of the verse melody may be hard to feel at first. Marvin Gaye sang it with some jazz phrasing. Though I've modified his version, I've included some of his phrasing. "Phrasing" means toying with the "as written" rhythm of the melody. Beginners may need to go phrase by phrase to memorize these more rhythmically complex lines.

Expansion Ideas

Once you learn Marvin Gaye's phrasing on "How Sweet It Is" you might want to try other phrasing ideas. Try entering each line of the song a little late to get used to singing slightly off the beat. This is called "back-phrasing." Also try hanging onto certain words a bit longer than you normally would, but not so much that there is no breathing room left at the end of the phrase. Phrasing is a great way to bring out important words in the lyric. Listen to Frank Sinatra and Billie Holiday to hear two masters of phrasing.

Check out their versions of "How Sweet It Is": Marvin Gaye • James Taylor

How Sweet It Is (to be Loved by You)

Brian Holland, Lamont Dozier & Eddie Holland

How sweet it is to be loved by you
How sweet it is to be loved by you

I needed the shelter of someone's arms
And there you were
I needed someone to understand my ups and downs
And there you were
With sweet love and devotion
Deeply touching my emotions
I want to stop and thank you, baby
I want to stop and thank you, baby

How sweet it is to be loved by you
How sweet it is to be loved by you

Close my eyes at night
And wonder what would I be without you in my life
Everything was just a bore
All the things I did, seems I'd done them before
But you brighten up all my days
With a love so sweet in so many ways
I want to stop and thank you, baby
I want to stop and thank you, baby

How sweet it is to be loved by you
How sweet it is to be loved by you

Since I Fell For You

<u>Focus:</u> Opening Highs, the Inner Smile
<u>Sound:</u> Nah
<u>Alto/Bass Key:</u> C
<u>Baritone/Soprano Key:</u> F

The nasal "nyeah" sound was used in "How Sweet It Is" to help smooth the transition between registers, and the open "yah" was used in "Willow Weep For Me" to get the open throat and soft palate lift that helps one attain relaxed high notes. "Nah" combines these two sounds. As you sing "nah" on "Since I Fell For You", you should feel nasal resonance and the soft palate lift, helping you to comfortably hit high notes.

A bit more on the soft palate: though at first it may feel like an involuntary muscle, you can learn to control it. A slightly raised soft palate will make all high notes easier to sing and improve your tone, whether the vowel is opened, closed or somewhere in-between. If you feel that you have no control over your soft palate, wait until the next time you yawn and feel the muscle lifting. Complete the yawn, then immediately do a yawn-sigh and try to replicate the feeling of lifting the soft palate. Don't worry if you don't get it right away, it can take several weeks. Another way to feel the lifting sensation is to inhale through your nose. With time and practice you'll be able to control the muscle and open the top back of your throat by lifting your soft palate at will. You'll know if you are over-lifting the palate: you'll sound like Kermit the Frog!

Ideally, you'll feel the soft palate lift slightly on a relaxed inhalation, then remain lifted as you sing on the exhalation. Additionally, the whole upper half of your face may feel like it's opening and lifting on the inhalation and exhalation. This facial + soft palate lifting is the "inner smile" that can help you both open up on high notes and control low notes. With the inner smile your face looks interested (but not surprised), and your upper throat feels open. You can slightly lift your eyebrows to help maintain the inner smile as you sing. There should be a sensation of opening and/or lifting in your nose and cheeks.

Every voice is different: you may feel that the high notes of "Since I Fell For You" fall in your chest, head or mix register. Wherever you feel them, you shouldn't feel any strain.

<u>Warming Up</u>
• Sing on "nah," feeling the inner smile. If you can't feel it with mouth inhalations, try nose inhalations.
• Sing the lyric, maintaining the inner smile.

Potential Trouble Spots and Hints

There's a lot of room to breathe on this song and you'll need the air, since there are many sustained notes as well as some high ones on the bridge. Many of the sustained notes are on diphthong vowels. Remember to sustain the open vowel of the diphthong; it will both feel and sound better. It wouldn't hurt to review the diphthong vowels in the "Unchained Melody" chapter and write the open vowel of each one above any sustained syllable. For instance, one of the first held words is "home," above that word on your lyric sheet write "aw"; that's the vowel you'll hang on when you hold the word out. Remember to sustain the vowel and not the consonant "m" on "home."

A brief digression on the "oh" vowel. Usually, there isn't a huge difference between how a vowel is spoken and how it is sung. There is, however, in the "oh" vowel. When speaking it most people don't drop the jaw or bring the lips forward. We can get away with this when speaking, but when singing, the vowel is extended and will sound too closed, especially on high notes. Because of this difference, it can take a bit longer to get the sung "oh" vowel to feel natural. Throughout each held "oh" you should focus on the "aw" vowel. Your lips should be forward and soft, not tight. Think like a fish. Watch that your tongue doesn't retract from its usual place just behind the lower teeth as your lips move forward.

The high notes of the bridge all fall on words with the "I" diphthong, which breaks into "ah-ee." Exploit that "ah" to open all the high notes, and make sure that your mouth is open enough. Feel free to not finish a phrase or switch from the lyric to "nah-nah" until you've mastered the high notes.

The start of the last line of the bridge, "I'm still in love with you," is a likely trouble spot. On high phrases that start with a vowel it's easy to grab at the word. This is called a "glottal attack." Put a subtle "h" at the beginning of the "I'm." It shouldn't be audible, but present enough so there's a bit of air cushioning your attack of the note.

Expansion Ideas

There's lots of room to ornament "Since I Fell For You" with neighboring tones, passing tones, and throbs. Phrasing can also be used to good effect. I've heard country, jazz, pop, and R&B versions of "Since I Fell For You." See how different fills and phrasing can take it in different stylistic directions: jazz versions often have fewer ornaments and more phrasing, country versions often have more descending passing tones, and R&B versions often have a bit of everything.

Check out their versions of "Since I Fell For You": Lenny Welch • Bonnie Raitt

Since I Fell For You

Buddy Johnson

When you just give love
And never get love
You'd better let love depart
I know it's so and yet I know
I can't get you out of my heart

You made me leave my happy home
You took my love and now you're gone
Since I fell for you

Love brings such misery and pain
I know I'll never be the same
Since I fell for you

Well it's too bad
And it's too sad
But I'm in love with you
Oh, you love me
Then you snub me
What can I do
I'm still in love with you

I guess I'll never see the light
I get the blues most every night
Since I fell for you
Since I fell for you

Dark End of the Street

Focus: Sustenance, Volume
Sounds: Le, Yeah, Wo
Alto/Bass Key: C
Baritone/Soprano Key: F

The two main differences between speaking and singing are that when you sing you hit specific pitches and must sustain them. Sustenance comes from coordinating and strengthening the breathing muscles (the diaphragm and abdominals) and the vocal cords. Good facial resonance will also help increase your sustenance. As the vocal cords become stronger they can hold a tone evenly for longer durations without tiring. However, they cannot do this without a continuous supply of air. The lungs are just sacks with no muscles; the diaphragm and adjacent muscles do the work of letting the air out slowly. My favorite sustenance exercise is the one described in the first chapter: take a deep breath, then let it out on "sss" to restrict the air flow, keeping your rib cage up. You'll feel your lower abdomen move in as the air goes out. Relax your throat as you inhale and you'll feel your diaphragm drop as your lungs fill. Try to work up to a count of thirty on each exhalation.

Warming Up

• Closed vowels use less air and your exhalation will last longer, so start "Dark End of the Street" on a "le."
• If your breath easily lasts to the end of each phrase switch to "yeah", and finally "wo."
• Switch to singing the lyric and see if you still have enough air to last through each phrase. Keep your rib cage up throughout and your throat relaxed, and with practice your sustenance will improve. If you find yourself running out of air by the end of a phrase, end the last note early until you build up your sustenance. You'll push from your throat if you hold on to the last note for dear life.

Potential Trouble Spots and Hints

Watch out for the lowest and highest notes. The "I" in the pick-up to the second verse ("I know that...") is the lowest note of the song. Don't over-open the "ah" in the "I" diphthong or you could lose your placement. When diphthongs are low in your range you can close up on them more without sounding swallowed.

The highest notes are in the bridge, all on the word "find." Now you can utilize the same "ah" in the long "I" diphthong vowel, since it's on a high note. Drop your jaw and loop the "nd" over to the "us": "They're gonna fah-ee ndus someday." That way you'll have maximum time on the open vowel.

Volume

Singing loudly too early in a warm-up can cause you to push your chest voice too high and strain. But at this point your voice should feel fairly elastic and resonant, so you can safely add some volume.

Increased volume comes from three places in the singing apparatus. Increased air pressure from your support muscles starts the crescendo. Your vocal cords must be strong enough to use the added air pressure correctly. If you've always been soft-spoken or have never sung with a lot of volume, your vocal cords need to be built up slowly. Gradually add volume to your singing and monitor your throat for any strain. You want to build the muscle here, not wear it out.

The third thing that helps to increase volume is facial resonance. I'm sure you've encountered people with naturally booming voices. Some people are born with sinus and mouth cavities that naturally resonate more than others. The rest of us can increase our resonance and volume by focusing the sound into and beyond these resonating chambers.

Increase your volume on "Dark End Of The Street" with each verse, singing "wo." Try to work standing up for this at first, you'll find it easier to breath and support the sound. Pick a spot across the room and focus on projecting your voice out through your eyes to that point. The inner smile can help, too. After you've sung the song, see if you feel any throat strain and if so, back off the volume a bit. If singing at this louder volume is comfortable for you, try singing the lyric. Try singing with more volume for the remaining workout songs, with the exception of "Save The Best For Last."

Expansion Ideas

The sustained notes in "Dark End Of The Street" give the singer lots of room for ornamentation. Try combining the neighboring tones and passing tones you experimented with on previous songs to make longer runs. To start, try double neighboring tones: sing a note, sing a step up, then return to your starting note. Immediately follow this by singing a step down, then return to the original note. A double passing tone is also a flashier fill: start on a note, sing down two notes and right back the same two notes up to the original note. Do these as fast as you can without losing the accuracy of the notes.

Check out their versions of "Dark End Of The Street": Linda Ronstadt · Ry Cooder

Dark End of the Street

Chips Moman & Dan Penn

At the dark end of the street
That's where we always meet
Hiding in shadows where we don't belong
Living in darkness to hide our wrong
You and me
At the dark end of the street
Just you and me

I know that time is gonna take its toll
We're gonna pay for the love that we stole
It's a sin and we know that it's wrong
But our love keeps coming on strong
You and me
At the dark end of the street
Just you and me

They're gonna find us
They're gonna find us
They're gonna find us someday
We'll steal away
To the dark end of the street
Just you and me

If you take a walk downtown
And you find some time to look around
If you should see me and I walk on by
Oh darling, please don't cry
Tonight we'll meet
At the dark end of the street
Just you and me
You and me

Walk Away Renee

<u>Focus:</u> Stepwise Pitch Work
<u>Sound:</u> De, Da
<u>Alto/Bass Key:</u> *A*
<u>Baritone/Soprano Key:</u> D

Once your highs feel open, your lows feel placed, and you've worked through any transitional bumps, you can focus on making sure that your pitch is accurate. I've only encountered two singers out of the over a thousand I've worked with who never sang out of tune. The rest of us need to continue to make pitch work a part of our singing regimen.

If you know that you have severe pitch problems, spend a lot of time singing the songs on Disc 1. Disc 2 has no melody to follow and will be much harder. Stay with the earlier, easier songs and sing them all on "de," which is an easier sound to control. You may need to work with a teacher if you can't tell when you are going out of tune. Taking a few piano lessons and spending time with a keyboard can also help those with major pitch problems. If you don't know, consult a professional and perhaps you'll be happily surprised; I've had numerous students come to me thinking they were tone-deaf who simply had to strengthen their voices, learn about placement, and focus a little more on listening.

Many singers can sing pretty much in tune but have occasional lapses. A number of factors can cause a singer to go off pitch. Straining for high notes can result in flatness, or singing lower than the intended note. Putting too much energy into reaching a high note can cause one to overshoot it and go sharp, or higher than the note. Not having placement and control of a low note can cause pitch problems, too. Singing with a loud band where you can't hear yourself can send you out of tune, as can listening only to yourself and not the other voices or instruments with which you are singing. Environmental factors and body changes can also affect pitch: women having their periods sometimes sing flat, as do people who haven't had enough sleep. Allergies can clog your sinuses and ears, changing how you resonate and affecting your hearing. Depressed people sometimes sing flat. Since the singer's instrument is his or her body, it is affected by many elements. As you learn about and strengthen your instrument, your sense of pitch can overcome many of these factors, but there may still be days when you have to focus on pitch a little more than others. If your sense of pitch seems to fluctuate a lot, analyze the factors that could be affecting it.

I've noticed in myself and many other singers that we will only go out of tune on certain vowels. These trouble vowels change from singer to singer. If you notice that you are out of tune on the same vowels from song to song ("uh" and "oh" are common ones), then after you've worked "Walk Away Renee" on "de" and "da," try it on "d"+ your problematic vowel. Try recording your voice if you aren't sure; it's easier to hear out-of-tune notes when they aren't coming from inside of you. I highly recommend recording yourself to help you polish your vocals. It doesn't have to be an expensive set-up for you to hear pitch or other vocal problems.

Working Pitch

• "De" is one of the easiest sounds to sing in tune, so start with that.

• If you're singing with Disc 1, listen to the voice to make sure your notes match, then listen to the piano to hear how the melody sits in the chords.

• If you're singing with the music-only track, focus on the piano. In general, piano is easier to tune to than guitar. You want to be able to hear yourself, but don't focus on your voice. Focus on the instrument to which you are tuning.

• If you can't hear yourself, try cupping a hand over one or both ears. Don't cover your ears, leave the front open. Or, if you have a portable CD player, move to another room that might be more reverberant, like a kitchen or bathroom.

• Forget about all the sliding from note to note that I've encouraged you to do up until now. Now you want your notes accurate. Watch for scoops, where you sing the note flat and then scoop up to the right pitch. Scoops are very common in most contemporary styles but you want to choose when to sing them, not sing them habitually.

• When the notes of the song are accurate *and* relaxed, sing an extended "de-ee" over each phrase of the song. This may be much harder, since the "d" helps you pinpoint each note.

• Now try the same process with "da" and an extended "da-a."

• Lastly, sing the lyric.

Potential Trouble Spots and Hints

The highest notes of the song are often the hardest, so watch out for the "away" of "Just walk away, Renee" and the "side" of "The empty sidewalk" in the chorus. "Way" and "side" both have diphthong vowels in them.

Many singers have their hardest time tuning half-steps, which in western music is the smallest interval between two notes. The first phrase of "White Christmas" is a good example of half-steps. Here are the first verse and chorus; the words are underlined where the half-steps occur:

<u>And when</u> I see <u>the sign</u> that points one way

<u>The lot</u> we used to <u>pass by</u> every day

Just walk <u>away</u> Renee

You won't see me fol<u>low you</u> back home

The emp<u>ty side walks</u> on my block are not <u>the sa</u>-a-ame

You're not to blame

As you learned from working with "da-da" then "da-a," it's harder to accurately sing a melisma, which is a vowel sound that covers more than one note.

Melismas occur on the words "home" and "eyes."

Expansion Ideas

When "Walk Away Renee" feels both flowing *and* accurate, put some emotion into the lyric. Work with dynamics: sing the verse softly, then increase in volume on the chorus. See if singing with emotion and dynamics affects your ability to stay in tune.

Check out their versions of "Walk Away Renee": The Left Banke • Vonda Shepard

Walk Away Renee

Mike Brown, Tony Sansone & Bob Calilli

And when I see the sign that points one way
The lot we used to pass by every day

Just walk away, Renee
You won't see me follow you back home
The empty sidewalks on my block are not the same
You're not to blame

From deep inside the tears that I'm forced to cry
From deep inside the pain that I chose to hide

Just walk away, Renee
You won't see me follow you back home
Now as the rain beats down
Upon my weary eyes
For me it cries

All of Me

Focus: Chromatic Pitch Work
Sounds: De, Da
Alto/Bass Key: F
Baritone/Soprano Key: C

You've probably noticed that some songs are harder to sing in tune than others. Obviously, songs with a wider range are tougher, but there are other factors as well. The melody of "Walk Away Renee" moves in what is called "stepwise motion," meaning there is either a half- or whole-step between any two consecutive notes, and the notes are all in the key of the song. Both these elements make it an easier song to sing than "All Of Me." In "All Of Me," the distance between two consecutive notes is often an interval of a third, and larger intervals are harder to sing accurately. The song also contains chromatic melodies. Chromatic melodies are melodies that include notes outside the key of the song and that move in half-steps. Notes that fall outside the key can strike you as dissonant (they sound like they clash with the chord) and therefore are harder to tune. And, as I noted in "Walk Away Renee," half-steps in general can be hard to sing in tune.

There's another element that might make this melody harder: not only are the intervals larger, but much of the melody descends. The vocal cords relax as you sing lower notes, and it's easy to overrelax and hit the note flat. Once again, "de" is an easier sound to control, so follow the same practice pattern that you followed on "Walk Away, Renee."

Working Pitch
• Sing the song on "de," then one extended "de-ee" per phrase.
• Do the same with "da," then "da-a."
• When the pitches are accurate, sing the lyric, noticing which words or vowels are harder to sing in tune.
• If you pinpoint certain notes as difficult ones, try aiming for the first consonant of the word on that note. Even though most consonants cannot be sustained, this approach can help you avoid pitch problems, particularly scoops.

Potential Trouble Spots and Hints
Every phrase of "All Of Me" has one or more of the difficult factors mentioned above. The first line "All of me, why not take all of me" is largely descending intervals of a major or minor third, as is much of the second line. The third line "Take my lips, I want to use them" starts with a chromatic descending line

followed by an ascending line of major and minor thirds. The rest of the song has similar movement, with the highest note on "All" of the final "All of me." So there are spots for potential pitch problems throughout the song. In general, on descending lines watch for over-relaxing each note and thereby going flat. Staying aware of placement on trouble words can help. On ascending lines make sure that you have enough breath support, and open each vowel the appropriate amount.

Expansion Ideas

As with "Walk Away Renee," once the notes are accurate you can add feeling and dynamics. "All Of Me" is also a fun song to phrase, so play with the rhythm a bit. Since this one is a pitch exercise, stay away from note variations.

Check out their versions of "All Of Me": Louis Armstrong • Billie Holiday

All of Me

Seymour Simons & Gerald Marks

All of me
Why not take all of me?
Can't you see
I'm no good without you?
Take my lips
I want to lose them
Take my arms
I'll never use them
Your goodbye
Left me with eyes that cry
How can I
Go on dear without you?
You took the part
That once was my heart
So why not take all of me?

Save the Best For Last

Focus: Adding Richness, Consonant Articulation
Sound: Duh, Nuh
Alto/Bass Key: Eb
Baritone/Soprano Key: Ab

You've probably noticed as you get into the higher songs of the workout that it takes no small effort to do it right. To sing high notes without straining requires the right balance of breath support, vocal strength, and placement. It should feel like your entire body is involved in your singing, not just your throat and lungs. At first, some of your higher notes may sound thin or weak to you. With practice, your vocal strength will increase and the sound will become fuller. Focus on how your voice feels, not how it sounds, when you are first increasing your range. It may feel like effort, but should never feel like strain.

Sometimes we overdo it when we're going for high notes. We start tightening our throats without realizing it, and the sound quality (or tone) becomes thinner. On "Save The Best For Last" you will again focus on facial resonance and tongue and throat relaxation to counter any tension that might have crept in as you have sung through the workout.

"Duh" is a very relaxed sound: the jaw drops halfway, the tongue relaxes and rounds, the mouth is in a neutral position, and subsequently the throat relaxes, too. Most of us get a richer, more resonant tone when singing "Duh." You can also try "Nuh," a similar but slightly more nasal sound.

Warming Up
• Sing "Save The Best For Last" on "duh" at a medium volume, noting the added richness in your tone. Notice how a richer tone can use more air, so watch your breathing and posture.
• Bring in your inner smile as you continue singing "Duh" so that your throat, jaw, and tongue are relaxed, while your soft palate, back of mouth, and upper half of your face feel open and lifted.
• Sing the lyric, trying to maintain a balance of relaxation and openness.
• Notice that when you are this relaxed and/or singing at a medium volume, your voice may move into an upper register at a lower pitch. Or you may notice that you can't tell where any register shifts are, it just feels like one big relaxed voice. This is a nice, elastic tone that works well in many contemporary styles, particularly on ballads.

Articulation

With "Save the Best for Last" you can now add crisp articulation to your list of concerns. In general, when singing any word the vowel is sustained and the consonant is pronounced lightly and crisply. Looping, discussed in the "Can't Help Falling In Love" chapter, gives you maximum time on the vowel. Concentration and practice are all that are needed to pronounce consonants clearly. We usually know how to do it, we just have to remember to do it.

Many of us have difficulty on only one or two consonants. Either you notice that your lips or tongue feel clumsy on a certain consonant, or you hear it (or more likely, notice the absence of it) as you listen to a recording of your singing. In that case, take the offending consonant or consonants and sing a whole song with them. For example, if "M" and "B" need work, try singing "mamba bamba" over the melody for "Save the Best for Last." Other frequently under-articulated consonants or consonant combinations are "v," "d," "n," "nd," and "ng." Under-articulation usually happens at the end of a word, and particularly in the last word of a phrase. You can also over-articulate a consonant; record and listen to yourself to see if you are overdoing it on certain consonants.

How much to articlulate consonants varies from style to style in contemporary music. Musical theater calls for very crisp articulation, while singing the blues calls for very relaxed articulation. Listen to different singers in your preferred style to get an idea of what's appropriate. For a ballad like "Save the Best for Last," I'd suggest clean but not overly crisp articulation.

Potential Trouble Spots and Hints

What's particularly difficult here is that some phrases end on high notes. It's much harder to gracefully complete a phrase on a high note than a low one. Technically, you'll approach those high notes in the usual supported, open manner. To complete the note you then have several artistic choices. You could end the note on the same volume with which you attacked it. Or, you could taper the volume down and do a quick fade. Make sure that your pitch stays true as you do this. Or, you could add vibrato to complete the note, with or without the volume fade. Check the "Can't Help Falling in Love" chapter for more help with developing a vibrato. All of these are legitimate ways to end a note. However, I would use the first method only if you are singing at a soft to medium volume. If you need to sing with a fair amount of volume to reach the high notes it might sound a bit abrupt in a ballad to simply end the note. That might fit better in a belted rock or show tune. Don't get discouraged if ending a phrase on a high note remains difficult for a long time. Many professional singers have the same difficulty and hide it by singing a passing tone or other ornament down to an easier lower note before ending the phrase.

<u>**Expansion Ideas**</u>

When Vanessa Williams recorded her pop version of "Save the Best for Last" she kept ornamentation and phrasing to a minimum. That kept the lyrics and melody front and center. If you want to take it in another stylistic direction, try adding descending passing tones to take it in a country direction, or phrase it to create a jazzier version.

Check out their versions of "Save the Best for Last": Vanessa Williams • Freddie Jackson

Save the Best for Last

Wendy Waldman, Jon Lind & Phil Galdston

Sometimes the snow comes down in June
Sometimes the sun goes 'round the moon
I see the passion in your eyes
Sometimes it's all a big surprise
'Cause there was a time when all I did was wish
You'd tell me this was love
It's not the way I hoped or how I planned
But somehow it's enough

And now we're standing face to face
Isn't this world a crazy place?
Just when I thought our chance had passed
You go and save the best for last

All of the nights you came to me
When some silly girl had set you free
You wondered how you'd make it through
I wondered what was wrong with you
'Cause how could you give your love to someone else
And share your dreams with me?
Sometimes the very thing you're looking for
Is the one thing you can't see

But now we're standing face to face
Isn't this world a crazy place?
Just when I thought our chance had passed
You go and save the best for last
You go and save the best for last

Sunny Came Home

<u>Focus:</u> Larger Melodic Leaps
<u>Sound:</u> Da
<u>Alto/Bass Key:</u> D
<u>Baritone/Soprano Key:</u> *G*

By now you have some knowledge of how to relax and open up high notes, and how to place and control low notes. Most of the songs so far consist of fairly gradual movement up and down. But some melodies contain larger and faster leaps that test the elasticity of your voice. Getting the feel for when to relax and when to control and place your voice comes with awareness and practice. In "Sunny Came Home," you'll be using all the techniques you've learned so far to help your voice stay elastic through some big melodic leaps.

<u>Warming Up</u>

You used the sound "da" earlier as a relaxation method. Now you'll be using it to build accuracy and elasticity, particularly on the chorus of "Sunny Came Home." Use the "d" to plant each note on the correct pitch. Use the open "ah" to stay relaxed.
• Sing the song on "da." Make the higher notes on "da" more open, the lower ones a bit more closed and nasal.
• To build accuracy, try to sing the melody without scooping up to the high notes. However, if any tension arises relax your voice and slide a bit. It's very easy to tense up when you start paying attention to pitch. Strive for a balance of accuracy and relaxation.
• Sing the lyric.

<u>Potential Trouble Spots and Hints</u>

It's the big leaps in the chorus where you'll want to be careful. Just as you did when singing the song on "da," drop your jaw on the high notes, then immediately close up a bit for the subsequent lows so they are very slightly nasal and placed in your face. Maintain good breath support throughout, especially for the high notes.

There are many diphthongs in the chorus, but don't worry about them when they fall on low notes. You can tone down everything I've said about diphthongs when they occur lower in your range. You can even lean on the closed half of the diphthong, which can help you place the note. On the high notes with diphthongs it's business as usual: find the open vowel and emphasize it. On the first line of the chorus those are the words "go," "I'm," and "no," so you'll focus on "aw," "ah," then "aw" again for the first three high notes. The "-king" of "walking" has a closed vowel on the high note. Part your teeth and lift your soft palate if it's difficult to reach.

The bridge sits around some low notes that will be easy for some to sing but may feel too low for others. Switch to "de" if the lows are hard to control, then when you switch back to the lyric go for a fair amount of nasal resonance. You can go fairly nasal without it sounding too honky when you're on low notes.

The bridge melody is very syncopated. That means that if you tap along with the beat the melody falls in-between your taps, on the upbeat. Syncopated rhythms can be harder to sing. Tapping while you sing can help you get used to the rhythm, and don't forget to breathe in-between each phrase.

Expansion Ideas

"Sunny Came Home" moves along at a healthy clip, so there's not as much room for ornamentation as on some of the other songs. For songs like this, another way to vary a melody is to substitute one alternate note per phrase: this can add variety as the song progresses without destroying the integrity of the melody. Substitution notes can add a subtle lift to a melody without being too showy. In a pop song you might not want to do this until after the first verse and chorus, when the melody has been established. For study purposes, however, I'll use the first verse. On the first line replace the melody note on "home" with a note that's one step higher. Substitute a note that's a fifth lower on "down" in the next phrase. Both these substitutions will still fit with the chord being played. Listen to the end of Disc 2 to hear these variations. By moving down in pitch on the word "down" you're demonstrating what the word means. It's always a good idea to keep the lyric in mind when doing note variations.

Check out the version of "Sunny Came Home" by Shawn Colvin

Sunny Came Home

Shawn Colvin & John Leventhal

Sunny came home to her favorite room
Sunny sat down in the kitchen
She opened a book and a box of tools
Sunny came home with a mission

She says, "Days go by I'm hypnotized
I'm walking on a wire
I close my eyes and fly out of my mind
Into the fire."

Sunny came home with a list of names
She didn't believe in transcendence
"Well, it's time for a few small repairs," she said
Sunny came home with a vengeance

She says, "Days go by I don't know why
I'm walking on a wire
I close my eyes and fly out of my mind
Into the fire."

Get the kids and bring a sweater
Dry is good and wind is better
Count the years you always knew it
Strike a match go on and do it

Days go by I'm hypnotized
I'm walking on a wire
I close my eyes and fly out of my mind
Into the fire
Oh light the sky and hold on tight
The world is burning down
She's out there on her own and she's alright
Sunny came home

Young At Heart

Focus: Putting It All Together
Sound: Yeah, Yah
Alto/Bass Key: F
Baritone/Soprano Key: Bb

The song after this one can be belted, so you'll want to make sure that your voice feels open, relaxed and strong before attempting the more aggressive belt style. "Young At Heart" is a great song for checking that, and the melody is tricky enough to challenge your ear at the same time.

Warming Up

Start with the sound "yeah"; as noted before, it's open enough to get the highs but closed enough to control the lows, and the nasality in the "y" helps to smooth any transitional bumps.
• Sing the melody on "yeah" until your voice feels elastic and the pitch is solid.
• Switch to the lyric. Run through this checklist to see if you are maintaining everything you've worked on in the workout:

1. Breathing and support: deep inhalations, rib cage up throughout
2. Relaxed face and throat, chin neither raised nor tucked down
3. Facial resonance
4. Awareness of simple vowels and diphthongs
5. The inner smile
6. Relaxed high notes and controlled low notes
7. Good intonation

Potential Trouble Spots and Hints

• Most of the phrases consist of one or two low notes a half-step apart which then leap to a high note. As with "Sunny Came Home," you'll be quickly moving back and forth from low to high. As always, control and place the lows, then open and support the highs. If you don't, the high or low notes may go flat. If you are singing some flat notes, borrow the sounds "me" and "mah" from "Wade In The Water." Sing those phrases as "Me me mah, me me mah.." until you've got them exact.
• If the notes go by too quickly for you to sing them accurately, you have two troubleshooting options. You can pause the CD and slowly practice those lines a cappella, gradually increasing speed as you repeat the lines. Or, sing the song with the music on Disc 2 and phrase the lines so that you move through the harder notes more slowly.

• Downplay the "r" in "hard" in the the fourth phrase, and on "worth" and "earth" on the first phrase of the last verse.
• Some high note diphthongs to stay aware of are: "Tales" (think "eh") on the first phrase, "know" (think "aw") on the first phrase of the second refrain, and "alive" (think "ah") just before the tag.

Expansion Ideas

In "Sunny Came Home" I talked about substituting one alternate note per phrase to vary the melody. Take that idea further and try altering an entire phrase. One way to alter a melody is to "invert" it. The melodic shape of the first two phrases of "Young at Heart" is:

```
       low low   high low low   high,  low low   high   low low high
   Fai - ry   tales can come  true,  it   can    hap - pen  to   you
```

To invert the melody, substitute high notes for all the low notes and vice-versa. The new melody will be quite different from the old, but will have the same rhythm and melodic shape, albeit turned upside-down.

Check out their versions of "Young at Heart": Frank Sinatra • Rosemary Clooney

Young At Heart

Carolyn Leigh & Johnny Richards

Fairy tales can come true, it can happen to you
If you're young at heart
For it's hard you will find to be narrow of mind
If you're young at heart
You can go to extremes with impossible schemes
You can laugh when your dreams fall apart at the seams
And life gets more exciting with each passing day
And love is either in your heart — or on the way

Don't you know that it's worth every treasure on earth
To be young at heart?
For as rich as you are it's much better by far
To be young at heart
And if you should survive to a hundred and five
Look at all you'll derive out of being alive
And here is the best part
You have a head start
If you are among the very young at heart

Crazy Baby

Focus: Belting
Sound: Yeah, Yah, Nah
Alto/Bass Key: Eb—G
Baritone/Soprano Key: Ab—C

    "Belting" is pushing the chest voice above the point where it would naturally shift to a higher register. It's a loud, full-voiced sound heard in all contemporary styles. It is also very hard on the vocal cords. It must be done consciously, with ample breath support, and only after you've built up a lot of vocal strength. It is very easy when working alone to cross the line from a supported belt to a strained belt, so proceed with caution. If you feel vocal fatigue during "Crazy Baby," do one of the following: 1) exclude the song until you have worked with the workout for at least two months, 2) work with a voice coach, or 3) stay in a mix or head register on the high notes. Sopranos and high tenors, with rare exceptions, will need to do the higher keys of "Crazy Baby" in a mix or the modified belt described in the next paragraph. Baritones, altos and basses *may* be able to belt all of the keys of the song in full chest voice or modified belt.

    It is very difficult to get from a high belted chest voice to a higher register without a break. Some styles, like country, incorporate the break. In other styles, the belting singer sings songs in a range where all the notes can be sung in the chest register. The safest and best approach is to do what I call a "modified belt" on the highs, where you blend in a bit of your mix. This gives you a sound that combines the openness of a chest tone with the "ring" of your upper register. The modified belt protects your voice and makes it easier to move to higher notes gracefully. Natalie Cole's and Celine Dion's high notes are good examples of this sound. While it is possible with time and training for most singers to develop a belt that can make a smooth transition to higher registers, this is fairly sophisticated work you may need to do with a voice coach.

    If you want to try working on your own, review the "How Sweet it Is" chapter and use the sound "nyeah" on higher notes. This nasal sound can help you move from a belt up into a modified belt or mix. Work full volume from the nasal "nyeah" towards an open "nah" sound, carefully monitoring your throat all the while for any sign of strain. To do this, try gently resting your fingers against your throat as you sing so you can monitor your larynx. If you strain as you belt your larynx will rise up. Try to keep it in a neutral position. Imagining that your larynx is moving forward as you sing can help. Make sure that your head also stays in a neutral position. Many belters mistakenly tilt their heads back, bringing extra tension to the throat. You will also lose resonance in your tone if you strain, so watch for that, too.

    Most of the vocal concepts already discussed come into play when belting.

Breath support, vowel awareness, facial resonance, and particularly the inner smile are important.

Belting "Crazy Baby"

You shouldn't have a problem with the first verse, chorus and second verse of "Crazy Baby," even though the second verse modulates up a half-step. If you do, sing it on "nah" or "yah" until it's comfortable, then switch to the lyric. On the first chorus, practice everything you'll need to belt the second chorus: stay aware of your support muscles, keep your throat relaxed, open the high vowels, maintain your inner smile and feel facial resonance.

The second chorus of "Crazy Baby" repeats several times, modulating to a higher key on each repeat.

• Sing these choruses on "yah" or "nah" as loudly as you comfortably can. If you have discovered another sound such as "wo" or "yeah" that is more comfortable for you, substitute that. Notice that the highest notes can be sung much louder than the lowest. That's the way the voice works: you can't get a lot of volume out of the low end of your range. You should feel facial resonance and no throat strain. Feel the slight lift of the soft palate, especially on the highest notes. Stay in chest voice if possible. Each higher note should resonate a little higher in your head, moving up from your soft palate and then arcing out through your eyes. If you feel strain on any of the repeat choruses, back off on the volume and bring in more of a mix or head register. Or, stop singing and don't try for any of the higher choruses until you've built up more strength. It will not strengthen your voice to push it when you feel strain.

• Switch to the lyric, but sing as if you are drunk, exaggerating the use of your mouth and jaw. This will help keep your throat relaxed and open while you get used to the lyrics.

• Sing the lyric, now with normal enunciation.

Potential Trouble Spots and Hints

All of the high notes in the chorus are on diphthongs. Remember to spend most of your time enunciating the first half of a diphthong when it falls on a high note. The note will be easier to sing and the pronunciation will fit the soulful style of the song. Therefore, emphasize "beh" on "ba-by," and "ah" on "tight" and "light." Slightly exaggerated use of the mouth and jaw can help you carry your chest voice higher. Watch belters as they sing high notes and see how much they open their mouths, even on closed vowels like "ee."

Expansion Ideas

If belting "Crazy Baby" becomes easy, have some fun with it. Virtually every ornamentation and phrasing idea I've mentioned so far can be used successfully here, particularly on the many sustained notes. Think about inflection on ornaments like passing tones and appoggiaturas: usually the first note is accented and the remaining notes are softer in volume.

Crazy Baby

Joan Osborne

And your hands are really shaking something awful
As you light your twenty-seventh cigarette
Oh how long have you been sitting in the darkness
You forget

Oh my crazy baby
Try to hold on tight
Oh my crazy baby
Don't put out the light
The light, the light, the light

Oh you know you're getting really hard to be with
And you're crying every time you turn around
And you wonder why you cannot pick your head up
Off the ground

Oh my crazy baby
Try to hold on tight
Oh my crazy baby
Don't put out the light

Oh my crazy baby
Try to hold on tight
Oh my crazy baby
Don't put out the light

Oh my crazy baby
Try to hold on tight
Oh my crazy baby
Don't put out the light

Oh my crazy baby
Try to hold on tight
Oh my crazy baby
Don't put out the light
The light, the light, the light

Song Study Order

Here are some areas to cover as you work on a song, in the order I usually use. The last few areas influence each other so there's no crucial order. Remember to check back with earlier items as you move along—it's easy, for example, to get wrapped up in style and forget about breathing.

1. <u>Notes:</u> Learn the notes as written before adding any variations.
2. <u>Rhythm:</u> Same as above for rhythm.
3. <u>Breathing:</u> Note where you're going to breathe on difficult phrases, and note any high or long passages where you'll want to support your voice with enough air.
4. <u>Placement:</u> Make sure you feel all notes resonating somewhere in your head, not your throat.
5. <u>Vowel Awareness:</u> Pronounce vowels correctly. This makes singing easier and better sounding.
6. <u>Intonation:</u> Make sure all notes are on the true pitch, neither flat nor sharp.
7. <u>Tone:</u> Is your tone right for the style of the song? Should it be clear, breathy, warm, edgy, or what?
8. <u>Attitude/Emotion:</u> What are you saying with the lyric? Does the emotion change as the song progresses? Without this element your song will be soulless.
9. <u>Stylizing:</u> Experiment with phrasing, runs, and dynamics. These are different tools to make the song your own and to put it across effectively.
10. <u>Stage Presence:</u> Does the rest of your body reflect what your voice is now putting across?

Some Ideas For Working on a Song

• Work with the lyric sheet even if you have it memorized. You can put in breath marks, pronunciation notes, dynamic markings, and emotional cues.

• Mark troublesome passages and review just those passages the next time you work on the song, before singing the entire song.

• Record yourself and analyze the results using this list.

• Jot down the main hurdles or reminders about the song, and scan them before singing the whole thing. Many singers will sing half the song before they remember what they'd figured out the day before.

• If you have several songs worked out to a performance or near-performance level, alternate between them so you have to approach each one fresh—you won't get to repeat a song on stage.

• If you get stuck, take a break: move around, stand on your head, or sing an easier song. Though you want to stay focused while singing it's easy for that focus to turn into subtle tension, Do what you can to stay both relaxed *and* aware.

Glossary

- <u>Diaphragm</u>: the muscle that works your lungs when you breathe.

- <u>Diphthong</u>: a combination vowel comprised of two simple vowels, an open vowel followed by a closed vowel. The mouth must move to pronounce it.

- <u>Glottal Attack</u>: a grabbing of the vocal cords that sometimes occurs when singing a word that begins with a vowel. Glottal attacks tire the voice.

- <u>Inner Smile</u>: a facial position where the soft palate is lifted and the sinuses are open. The upper half of the face feels open and lifted.

- <u>Larynx</u>: the voice box in the throat where the vocal cords are found.

- <u>Looping</u>: carrying the last consonant in a word over to the next word to maximize time on the vowel and make one's singing more flowing.

- <u>Melisma</u>: a vowel sound that lasts for more than one note. Runs are usually melismas.

- <u>Ornamentation</u>: a one- to four-note addition to a note. Here are the basic ornamentations, written in numeric form, e.g.: in the key of C:
C=1, D=2, E=3, F=4, G=5, A=6, B=7, C=8:
<u>Neighboring tone</u>: a step away in either direction, then a return to the first note. 121, 565, 878, 323, etc.
<u>Appoggiatura</u>: singing one step above the desired note, then resolving down. 43, 21, 65, etc. Less common are upward resolving appoggiaturas, usually sung in the blues.
<u>Passing tone</u>: A descent or ascent from the note in stepwise motion to the next note that fits the chord. This will always be two or three steps away. 321, 543, 5678, 345.
<u>Throb</u>: a double attack on a note, using a surge of air. 88, 33, 11 etc.
<u>Alternate chordal note</u>: A jump of a third or a fourth to the nearest note that also belongs in the chord being played. One can sing the melody note then go to the alternate chordal note, or skip the melody note and go right to the alternate. 31, 135, 853, etc.
I sing examples of all these ornaments at the end of Disc 2.

- <u>Pentatonic Scale</u>: a five note scale based on the natural minor scale. Fragments and variations of the pentatonic scale are often used for runs. Numerically, the notes are: 1 , b3, 4, 5, b7. In the key of A, for example, the pentatonic scale would be A, C, D, E, G.

- <u>Phrasing</u>: singing the same notes of a given melody while altering the rhythm.

- <u>Placement</u>: feeling the voice vibrate in the resonators in the head: the mouth, nose, cheekbones, and around the eyes.

- <u>Range</u>: all of the notes a singer can sing.

- <u>Register</u>: different areas of the voice that make up the entire range. Singers are commonly thought to have two or three registers: head and chest; or head, mix, and chest.

- <u>Resonance</u>: the bouncing of vibrating air against different parts of the body, creating the vocal sound. When singing correctly one feels resonance in various parts of the head and sometimes the chest. Though the vibration starts in the throat, sensations of too much throat resonance can lead to vocal fatigue.

- <u>Run</u>: an extended ornamentation added to the melody, also called a riff or fill.

- <u>Scoop</u>: a slide up to a note.

- <u>Simple Vowel</u>: a vowel that can be pronounced with your mouth in one position.

- <u>Soft Palate</u>: the back of the roof of the mouth, directly behind the hard palate. The soft palate lifts when you yawn.

- <u>Vocal Cords</u>: Muscle folds, surrounded by tissue and a mucous membrane, through which air passes, causing a vibration that resonates in the body and becomes the voice.

About the Author

Susan Streitwieser Anders, MA, has coached singers for over twenty years. Her articles on singing have appeared in Acoustic Guitar, Acoustic Musician, Backstage West and numerous internet sites. Susan's *No Scales, Just Songs Vocal Workout Volumes One and Two* have been used by singers worldwide, as have her *Harmony Singing By Ear CDs. Singing With Style*, Susan's jazz warm-up and vocal style CD set, is her newest project.

Susan has recorded five albums with her band Susan's Room: *Susan's Room, Lion in the Living Room, Thicker, Thinner*, and *Room #5*. As a solo artist she has recorded two albums: *You Can Close Your Eyes Lullabies*, and *Release*. Susan grew up in Berkeley, California and now lives in Nashville, Tennessee.

Produced and Engineered by Tom Manche at Studio X in Los Angeles, CA

The Band
Vocals: Susan Anders
Vocals: Geoffrey Tozer
Keyboards: Troy Dexter
Bass: Ritt Henn & Bill von Ravensberg
Drums: Albe Bonacci
Guitar: Tom Manche

CD Track Lists

Disc 1

1) Introduction
2) Angel From Montgomery Intro
3) Angel From Montgomery
4) Centerpiece Intro
5) Centerpiece
6) Sweet Dreams Intro
7) Sweet Dreams
8) Wade in the Water Intro
9) Wade in the Water
10) I'll Stand By You Intro
11) I'll Stand By You
12) Unchained Melody Intro
13) Unchained Melody
14) Can't Help Falling in Love Intro
15) Can't Help Falling in Love
16) Willow Weep for Me Intro
17) Willow Weep for Me
18) How Sweet It Is Intro
19) How Sweet It Is
20) SinceI Fell for You Intro
21) SinceI Fell for You
22) Dark End of the Street Intro
23) Dark End of the Street
24) Walk Away Renee Intro
25) Walk Away Renee
26) All of Me Intro
27) All of Me
28) Save the Best for Last Intro
29) Save the Best for Last
30) Sunny Came Home Intro
31) Sunny Came Home
32) Young at Heart Intro
33) Young at Heart
34) Crazy Baby Intro
35) Crazy Baby

Disc 2

1) Angel From Montgomery
2) Centerpiece
3) Sweet Dreams
4) Wade in the Water
5) I'll Stand By You
6) Unchained Melody
7) Can't Help Falling in Love
8) Willow Weep for Me
9) How Sweet It Is
10) Since I Fell for You
11) Dark End of the Street
12) Walk Away Renee
13) All of Me
14) Save the Best for Last
15) Sunny Came Home
16) Young at Heart
17) Crazy Baby
18) Stylizing Examples